GREAT PEACEMAKER

Reconstructed and Illustrated by Ari Idee

Great Peacemaker by Ari Idee

Copyright © 2013 Technology and Imagination Press
Text and Illustrations Copyright © 2013 by Ari Idee
All rights reserved.

No part of this publication may be reproduced, stored in a retrieval system, or transmitted
in any form or by any means, electronic, mechanical, photocopying, recording,
or otherwise, without written permission of the publisher.
For information, on getting permission for reprints and excerpts,
contact tip_books@happyhippocreations.com

ISBN: 0-9798991-3-3
ISBN-13: 978-0-9798991-3-3
First Printing 2013

A long time ago, close to Lake Ontario, the border between Canada and the current state of New York of the United States, the Haudenosaunee people lived together in connected villages. These American Indian people lived in long houses constructed of elm saplings and bark.

The women planted seeds and harvested abundant crops of "the three great sisters" – corn, beans and squash. The men hunted and fished. As the adults worked, children laughed merrily in the cornfields.

Birds chirped throughout the surrounding forests.
The breeze rustled the leaves and clouds drifted across the deep blue sky.
This is how the Haudenosaunee people lived. They were a group of people who lived in peace with Mother Nature.
This peaceful life was a gift from their ancestors, Hiawatha of the Onondaga and Deganawida of the Wendat.

The Haudenosaunee people were composed of five tribes: the Mohawk, Oneida, Onondaga, Cayuga, and Seneca peoples. Originally, these groups lived in separate territories. They fought all the time over fishing areas and hunting places. If a tribe was attacked, they attacked back.

Many warriors lost their lives.
All the women grieved.
Children feared even the whisper of leaves.

Deganawida, who was called the "Great Peacemaker," was raised as a Wendat. This tribe lived north of Lake Ontario. As a man of the Wendat, a tribe of fierce warriors, Peacemaker was a black sheep. He didn't want to go to war. He wanted all people to live in peace. Even though Peacemaker always tried to talk the Wendat people out of all their fighting, they would just look at him strangely and shake their heads.

Peacemaker decided to leave the Wendat to talk to other tribes. "Maybe other tribes will listen to me more than my own people do," he thought. On the day he left the Wendat territory, he said goodbye to his mother and grandmother. He made a promise to them. "I will go to stop our brothers fighting each other. We are all human beings. Why do we have to hurt each other?"

Because he could not convince his own people, Peacemaker set out on Lake Ontario with his canoe toward the easternmost tribe, the Mohawk people. When he landed, he sat down at the edge of the forest and smoked his pipe. Visitors nearing the village of a different tribe customarily smoked a pipe of tobacco. The smoke let the people of the village know the visitor was not an enemy.

Soon after, Mohawk men came to him and led him to their chief. Peacemaker introduced

himself and said, "I am here to bring the gift of peace to your people. From now, we will stop fighting with other tribes."

One man, sitting close to a listening elder, criticized Peacemaker's words by saying, "If we don't attack them, they will attack us. We must do it or die ourselves."

Peacemaker answered his words quietly to that man. "Every tribe has the same fear. What if we knew that no tribe would hurt ours? No one needs to attack anyone. We need to unite all the neighboring tribes to live in peace. We are all brothers. We can unite into a confederacy."

While Peacemaker was trying to convince the Mohawk people to accept his idea of a confederacy, one Mohawk woman went to get water. As she approached the shore of the lake she found a strange man sitting there. His head was drooping and he was wearing strings of white shells. This news spread quickly around the meeting of the Mohawk people and Peacemaker.

Peacemaker told the people to bring the man near the counsel because white shells were a sign of friendship and peace. Soon, some Mohawk men brought the man into the village. This stranger looked weary and sorrowful.

Peacemaker rose and stepped near to the man. He said, "My brother, I believe you left your own land to come here. I did too. I am here to bring the gift of peace. What brought you here?" The man gazed quietly at Peacemaker for a moment, then he started talking about himself slowly.

"I am Hiawatha. I am from the tribe of the Onondaga. I used to be a warrior but I don't want to fight with anyone anymore.

My village has a warrior chief named Tadodaho, who loves war." Even though Hiawatha had tried hard to convince Tadodaho to end his evil path, he was not successful. In the same period of time, Hiawatha's beloved daughters died in quick succession. This loss killed any possibility of joy in his life completely. Wandering around, lost in his grief, he drifted into the land of the Mohawks.

Deeply sympathizing with Hiawatha, Peacemaker entreated him to stay in the Mohawk village with him. Hiawatha accepted his offer.

When Peacemaker was about to fall asleep that night, he heard Hiawatha sobbing near a pole strung with three strings of beads. Hiawatha was talking to himself: " If I saw anyone who was burdened with grief due to a loss of a beloved person, I would console him with these strands. These beads can become words and lessen the darkness in which he is living."

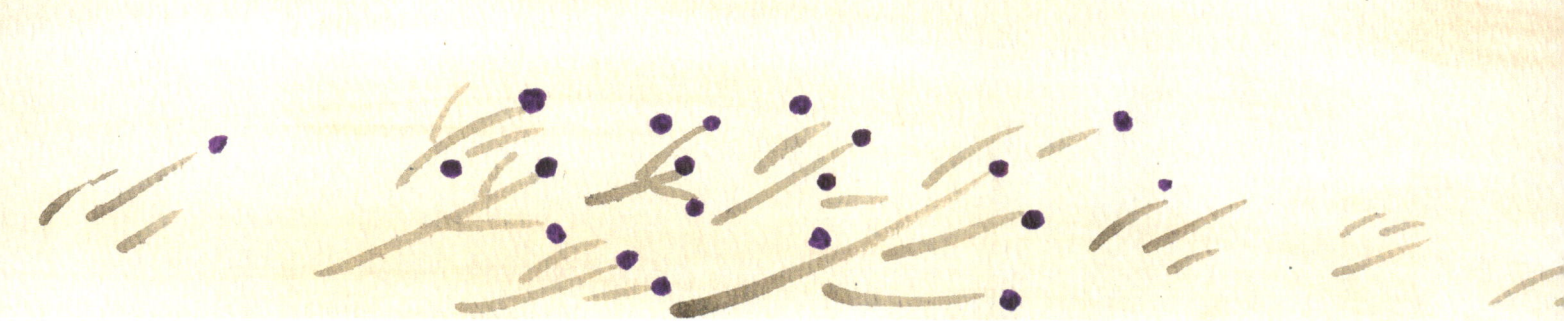

    Peacemaker approached Hiawatha and took these strands of beads into his hands. Giving one string to Hiawatha, he said, "When people suffer that greatest loss caused by death, their eyes are glued shut by tears. I will wipe away your tears." Giving him the second string, Peacemaker said, "When people suffer that greatest loss caused by death, their ears cannot listen due to their grief. I will unplug your ears." And, giving him the third string, Peacemaker said, "When people suffer that greatest loss caused by death, their throats are choked with grief. I will open your throat."
    As Peacemaker finished saying these words, Hiawatha's eyes, ears and throat healed and his mind became clear and straightened.

    Peacemaker told Hiawatha that he was traveling to convince the neighboring tribes to form a confederate league. Hiawatha shared Peacemaker's feeling of making peace with neighboring tribes. Mohawks now accepted their plan for the confederacy.

    Then Peacemaker and Hiawatha carried their message to the Oneida tribe, nearest to the Mohawks. The Oneida chief finally accepted the plan after a year of talks.

    Next they visited the Onondaga tribe, Hiawatha's home from which he left because of the oppressive leader, Tadodaho. As expected, Tadodaho refused the confederacy plan with a sneer.

    Even though they could not convince the Onondaga war chief, Tadodaho, they didn't lose their determination to form a confederate league.
    They left the Onondagas and traveled to the Cayugas, the tribe that was always defeated by their neighbors, the Onondagas. The Cayuga people accepted the confederacy plan quickly with great relief. Peacemaker and Hiawatha moved on to take their ideas to the Senecas. There they learned from the Seneca chief that there was a conflict between people who were willing to accept the confederacy plan and a warrior leader, with some followers, who was not. Peacemaker left the chief to convince the warrior leader and went back to the Onondaga tribe with Hiawatha again.

When Peacemaker and Hiawatha returned to the Onondaga lands, the friends were shocked at Tadodaho's appearance. His evil heart had even attracted snakes. Many of them clung to his head by his hair. He even stared with a cold-blooded look of ice in his eyes.

Hiawatha gently picked snakes, one by one, out the tangle of them in Tadodaho's hair. As the snakes detached from Tadodaho, he seemed more and more relaxed and warmer.

But when Peacemaker talked to him about the need to stop wars and unite with the neighboring nations, Tadodaho stood his ground.

"If I don't attack them first, I will be attacked," he shouted at them. But Peacemaker spoke with him quietly. "Every tribe has had this same fear. That is why I am here – to stop the cycle of

violence. If we all were in the same league, we would know that we would never attack our brothers in the league with us, so no one would need to fear any attack." Tadodaho looked surprised for just a moment. Then, quickly he replied to Peacemaker, "We are known as the brave Onondagas. We are proud of our strength. We must show this strength to the other tribes." Peacemaker nodded, then said, "It's time for you and your warriors to be brave enough to avoid wars now."

    Tadodaho's eyes sprang open as Peacemaker continued, "You attack others not because of your bravery but because of your fear. If you were afraid of no one, you could show all the nations that you have ceased attacking your neighbors because you fear no one. This is real bravery and strength."

The last of the snakes dropped from Tadodaho's deeply bowed head. The Onondaga people anxiously watched him. They badly wanted Tadodaho to accept this offer of a path to peace. They had had enough of the life of war.

Tadodaho looked at his people, the Onondagas. He saw how many children were in the village as if it was his first time to really see them. While he was in the midst of the battle – which had been his daily life for a long time – he never gave a single thought to the children. "When was the last time I saw children playing in this village?" he thought to himself. He began to reminisce about his own childhood. He remembered playing in the cornfields with the other boys. The mothers and girls worked amongst the growing crops, chatting and softly laughing. He closed his eyes. "How did I forget those happy days, the blue sky, the boys together laughing, and the scent of the three sisters growing in the summer heat?" he asked himself.

 He remembered how he had played games with the other boys so hard all the day, until he smelled his mother's delicious supper in the pot, and then he ran toward his home…..
 Tadodaho felt the sun's warmth on his cheeks. He missed those days. He had spent his adulthood as a brave warrior chief protecting his people, but somehow or other he now found himself afraid even of his own people.
 "It's too late for me to change,." he said. Hiawatha took Tadodaho's fist in both of his own two hands. "We are brave and proud Onondagas. Let us bravely display our painful and bloody past. Even though it is ugly, we will offer it to our elders and ask forgiveness, and to our children, who will learn from their fathers." Tadodaho nodded his tear-streaked face. Now, the Onondaga people could also accept the offer of confederacy.

While Peacemaker was gazing at the changed Tadodaho quietly, he received a message from the Seneca people. The Seneca nation had accepted the plan of confederacy.
Peacemaker stood up and called to Hiawatha to come near.

Then he whispered to Hiawatha, "I have an announcement to make to everyone!" When he heard what had happened, Hiawatha was overjoyed. He shouted for all to hear, "My brothers! We have a league! Five nations are now united in our confederacy. There will be no more wars in this league!" Great shouts of joy arose from the crowds.

Five Nations were in the league now. Peacemaker planted a pine tree where Tadodaho had experienced his great change of heart. No matter how filled with bad spirit a person is, each person can choose a new path and redeem his or her mind. This now sacred location was the only place that they could hold their official conferences. Chiefs of the Five Nations would sit under this pine tree to hold their meetings forever, symbolized by this pine which is forever green.

Peacemaker chose a symbol for the confederacy. He drew a pine tree with four large roots. These roots were stretched into the four directions to symbolize that in all directions (the Four Corners of the Earth) there will be peace. Other Nations, such as the Tuscarora around 1722, could join this powerful confederacy and they could be protected under this tree. On top of the tree, an eagle was guarding the peace of the Haudenosaunee people. Under the tree, weapons of war were buried. Peacemaker hoped they and their descendants would never need those weapons ever again, for all time.

They were the Haudenosaunee, people with the wisdom shared by the five nations, people who lived in peace with Mother Nature. Children played in the cornfields.

Women worked busily in their fields with "the three great sisters." Men hunted and fished together in the shared grounds, and came back home safely. All the members of this confederacy built up a good life of peace and happiness.

About 200 years after Peacemaker brought the original five tribes that made the Haudenosaunee together, the new world colonies that would become the United States declared their independence from England and the taxes imposed by King George. Benjamin Franklin and Thomas Jefferson, members of the drafting committee for this Declaration of Independence, researched around the world for a high-minded model of government to rule this new land that would be worthy of the United States of America. They consulted with the Haudenosaunee people about their confederacy of six "nations." Their cooperative governing system, especially the principle of ruling by majority vote, influenced Franklin and Jefferson as they started to write the rules that would become the Constitution of the United States of America.

The symbol of the Haudenosaunee confederacy, a noble eagle, was also shared as the national bird of the United States of America. Haudenosaunee people spoke openly about their way of life, showing that all men are brothers. In this way they influenced the world's first practicing democracy.

Listen to Peacemaker
Follow his whisper

Hold hands, not weapons
Let's talk, not attack
What matters our difference?
What matters our appearance?

Pines don't fight Maples for water
Eagles don't slay Vultures from bias
Only Humans hurt others for gain
Only Humans wound Humans who differ

We are the same children
Children of the mother earth
Children of the father sky

Hold hands, not weapons
Let's talk, not attack

Ari Idee was born in Japan in 1976. She graduated with a B.A. in Art from Ueno Gakuen University in 1999 and a B.A in English Literature from Meiji Gakuin University in 2003.

http://aribooks.com

www.ingramcontent.com/pod-product-compliance
Lightning Source LLC
Chambersburg PA
CBHW041226040426
42444CB00002B/68